AUSTRALIAN ABORIGINAL CULTURE

prepared by
Australian InFo International

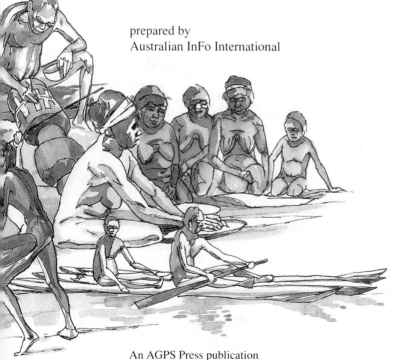

An AGPS Press publication
Australian Government Publishing Service
Canberra

Reprinted 1991
Reprinted 1993

The National Library of Australia Cataloguing-in-Publication data:

Australian Aboriginal Culture.
  3rd ed.
  Bibliography.
  ISBN 0 644 09814 7.
  [1]. Aborigines, Australian, I. Australian
  InFo International.
306.0899915

Illustration Acknowledgments
Many of the illustrations in this text have been reproduced from *Australian Aboriginal Culture,* first published in 1973. Credits for these illustrations remain unchanged. Additional illustrations have been reproduced by kind permission of the Australian Institute of Aboriginal Studies (AIAS); Australian InFo International (AII); Australian Overseas Information Service (AOIS); National Library of Australia (NLA); Commonwealth of Australia (CA); and private individuals.

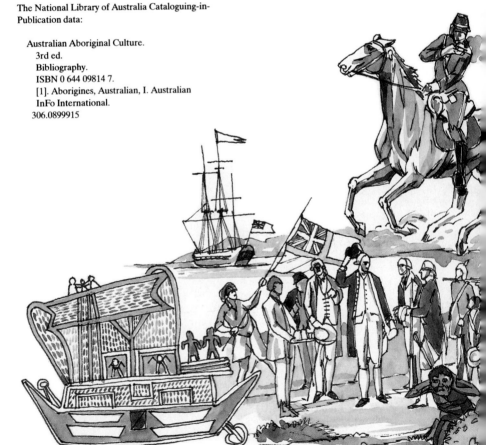

Typeset in Australia by CPN Publications
Printed in Australia by R. M. LANSDOWNE, Commonwealth Government Printer

Contents

Preface

The genesis of this publication dates back to 1949 when the Unesco General Conference decided to promote mutual understanding between nations by the exchange of cultural exhibitions prepared by member States.

The Australian contribution, through Australian Government funding and the work of the Australian National Commission for Unesco, resulted in a travelling exhibition on Aboriginal Australia and the brochure *Australian Aboriginal Culture* (1953). The work was carried out by the then Curator of Anthropology, Fred McCarthy of the Australian Museum. More than 100 000 copies of the brochure were sold.

A new edition of the brochure was published in 1973 and was prepared by Robert Edwards, the then Deputy Principal of the Australian Institute of Aboriginal Studies. It was reprinted in 1974. The demand for the publication has increased each year and reflects the growing wave of interest both within Australia and around the world in the people who are the heirs of the oldest continuing civilisation on earth.

Concurrent with the expansion of interest has been the march of knowledge. Even the most recent revision of this publication gave 30 000 years as the probable length of time Aboriginal Australians have occupied the continent.

We now know that Aboriginal people have lived in Australia for more than 40 000 years and quite likely for much longer. Various estimates were made of the Aboriginal population at the time of the arrival of the First Fleet in 1788. A figure of 300 000 was accepted for many years but more recent research has indicated that the figure was somewhere between 500 000 and a million people.

Similarly, a present-day population figure in the 1973 edition of *Australian Aboriginal Culture* estimated there was a total of over 106 000 Aboriginal people in Australia. The latest census figures indicate the population as being around 227 645.

This new version of *Australian Aboriginal Culture* brings together not only information on present-day Aboriginal and Torres Strait Islander life but also looks at the past 200 years in the light of historical re-evaluation. The book also sets out to show the continuity of Aboriginal culture as it has survived over thousands of years. Today traditional beliefs, values and lifestyles are thriving in many traditional communities. Furthermore, there is a resurgence of culture among Aboriginal people in urban environments and those living outside traditional areas who, nowadays, make up the majority of the Aboriginal population.

The dramatic growth of knowledge about Aboriginal culture has been matched by the pace of development of Aborigines and Torres Strait Islanders. This is a pace set by and for themselves and which the Australian Government is seeking to support.

The whole of the national infrastructure serving Aboriginal affairs is in the process of reorganisation and the Aboriginal and Islander communities themselves are engaged in planning their futures.

During the bicentennial year of 1988 thousands of Aborigines and Torres Strait Islanders gathered in Sydney for the largest assembly of first Australians known in their history on this continent. It was a triumph of their organisation from every State and Territory and was a symbol of their determination to defend and strengthen their ancient culture and heritage.

Marji Hill
Project co-ordinator
Australian InFo International

1 A traditional owner, Uluru (AOIS)

2 A broadcaster at an Aboriginal radio station in Alice Springs (AOIS)

3 Margaret Major, a Kalkadoon from Mount Isa (AII)

Two separate groups of people make up the original Australians. These are the Aborigines and the Torres Strait Islanders.

Prior to 1788, Aborigines occupied all of mainland Australia and most of the inhabitable islands near the coast, including Tasmania. 'Aborigines' was not the name these people used to describe themselves. The term 'Aborigines' was given to the first Australians by the Europeans because it means the original inhabitants of the country. Aborigines used and still use the names applicable to their own groups. For instance, today's Aborigines are likely to call themselves by the name of the language or territory group to which they belong — Wiradjuri, Pitjantjatjara, Kamilaroi, Gurnai, Aranda. Also they may use a general term like Murri, Koori, Nunga, Nyoongah or Yolgnu. Torres Strait Islanders use the name of their island community — Badu, Murray, Yam, Boigu.

The Torres Strait Islands lie in the Torres Strait which is the stretch of water that separates Cape York Peninsula in north Queensland from Papua New Guinea. The people from these islands form the second group of the original Australians.

The Original Australians

Aboriginal people

Today the Aboriginal population of Australia numbers around 227 645 people, about 1 1/2 per cent of the total Australian population of about 16 million. Prehistorians such as D.J. Mulvaney (1989) put the Aboriginal population in 1788 as somewhere between 500 000 and a million people, although modern estimates have ranged from 300 000 to 3 000 000. What is certain is that the coming of the British in 1788 was the beginning of a rapid decrease in the Aboriginal population in areas where Aboriginal and British people came into contact. Warfare between Aboriginal people and the British, together with the diseases the British introduced, accounted for this rapid population decrease.

It is difficult to provide statistics of Aboriginal Australians who died as a result of warfare with the British but one historian, Henry Reynolds (1981), estimated the Aboriginal casualties in north Australia above the Tropic of Capricorn as exceeding 10 000. This is twice the number of white Australians from the same area killed in foreign wars between the outbreak of the Boer War and the end of the Vietnam War.

A lot of people who have written or spoken about Aboriginal people in the past have referred to their way of life as 'primitive' or have described their culture as inferior. Associated with this idea of a 'stone age' culture is the image of 'naked hunters' and 'food gatherers' of the arid deserts of Central Australia. This is a very superficial and rather inaccurate picture of both present-day and past Aboriginal life. Today's Aborigines live with other Australians in main cities, country towns and rural areas. They are to be found in State parliaments, in the professions and in the top levels of business and government administration. Others are making national and international reputations in the arts, literature and sport.

Throughout the country many Aboriginal communities are living on land that has been given back to them by the government. These lands may have been former mission or government reserves on which several generations of families traditionally lived.

Official government policy says that any person who is of Aboriginal descent, who is recognised as such by other Aboriginal people and who recognises himself or herself as Aboriginal is, in every sense, Aboriginal. In this definition the degree of descent from Aboriginal parents is irrelevant.

According to the 1986 Census, Queensland has the largest population of Aborigines and Torres Strait Islanders with 61 268, then New South Wales with 59 011, Western Australia with 37 789, Northern Territory with 34 739, South Australia with 14 291, Victoria with 12 611, Tasmania with 6716 and the Australian Capital Territory with 1220.

4 Lin Onus, artist from Victoria (Neil McLeod)

1

Torres Strait Islanders

The Torres Strait Islands remained under joint British and Queensland colonial control until 1879. In this year an Act was passed in the Queensland Parliament bringing all the Torres Strait Islands under Queensland authority. Queensland continues to administer the islands following the recent redrawing of the border between Queensland and Papua New Guinea.

Torres Strait Islanders are of Melanesian descent and according to tradition the islands were occupied by voyagers from Papua New Guinea.

Originally, New Guinea and Australia formed one extensive continent whose earliest inhabitants were ancestors of today's Aborigines. With the rising of the seas at the end of the last Ice Age, around 15 000 years ago, New Guinea was separated from Australia leaving the crests of the mountains as islands in the western Torres Strait and the tops of volcanoes forming the eastern islands. Gradually a new Melanesian population was established in New Guinea, which in turn began to populate the islands of the Strait. Only the people in the western islands closest to the Australian coast retained links with the mainland Aborigines.

There are no records of the size of the population of the Islands prior to the initial contact in 1606 with the European ships, and later British merchant ships which began to use the Torres Strait more and more in the early 19th Century. However, it is clear that from the time the Europeans came the population of the Torres Strait began to decline. This is mainly because of the diseases the ships brought with them and a series of violent battles fought between ships' crews and the Islanders.

Today there are about 22 000 Torres Strait Islanders, although only 5000 live on the Torres Strait Islands themselves. The rest reside in Australia, mainly in Queensland.

6

7

8

5 The Torres Strait Islands (CA)

6 Islands in the Torres Strait (AOIS)

7 Boy from Badu Island (AOIS)

8 Thursday Island girl (AOIS)

9 Dancer from Badu Island (AOIS)

9

[Map]

PAPUA NEW GUINEA

Boigu
NORTH WESTERN
ISLANDS Dauan
Buru
Saibai
Stephen EASTERN
ISLANDS
CENTRAL
ISLANDS Damut Darnley
Tutu Yorke Murray
Yam Dauar
Mabuiag Aurid Waier
Badu
WESTERN Bet Coconut
ISLANDS Moa Sue
Nagir
Wara
Hammond Thursday
Horn Mt. Aldolphus
Prince of Wales Aibany
Possession
CAPE YORK
PENINSULAR
Great Barrier Reef
N
0   50
Km

5

2

History of Australia (pre-1788)

Aboriginal religious tradition places the origin of each Aboriginal clan in its own land. Central to Aboriginal religious beliefs are the ancestral creative beings who shaped the land and created the plants, reptiles, insects, fishes, birds and people. These ancestral creative beings journeyed across the continent in the Dreamtime; they emerged from the subterranean or heavenly world and moved over the featureless earth. The places where they first appeared and the land that they covered on their journeys became the billabongs and rivers, the rocks, hills and mountains, and all the features of the environment. At the same time, the ancestral creative beings placed in this setting all of life, human, animal and plant, in an interconnected system of relationships. This done, they retired — to the sea, underground or to the heavens, although they have never really abandoned their creations. Their creative forces are still active in the land and may be summoned and revitalised through the performance of a cycle of rituals. Although invisible, the ancestral creative beings remain a vital force that have the power to intervene in the lives of the animals and people they have created.

The first histories of Australia may be found in this body of religious law. Many Aboriginal people today believe that their early ancestors originated in the continent. Gradually, archaeological research is unveiling the story of the earliest Australian people from a scientific perspective. Dates for human occupation of the continent have been claimed to go back 100 000 years. These very early dates have not been confirmed but recent evidence indicates the presence of people near Sydney using stone tools over 40 000 years ago (Nanson, Young and Stockton 1987). It is reasonable

to claim then that Aboriginal people have been making Australia their home for at least 45 000 to 50 000 years .

If the first Australians did not originate in Australia where did they come from? Archaeological knowledge is sparse on this question but it is commonly believed that they came from South East Asia and that they came by sea. These first sea voyages, whether they were deliberate or accidental, were less than 100 kilometres. As for the pattern of migration prehistorians have yet to agree. While some have the theory that there were two migration periods others say that there was only ever one.

Throughout the 45 000 years or more that Aboriginal people have been on the

10

10 Excavations at Kintore Cave, Northern Territory, provide evidence of early human life in Australia (D.A. Casey)

3

continent, they have had to adapt to dramatic changes in their environment caused by changes in climate and movement of landmasses. The drowning of the land between Australia and New Guinea marked the gradual ending of an ice age which had continued, in varying degrees of intensity, from about 80 000 to 7000 years ago. During all that time sea levels varied but, generally, they were much lower than they are now and the landmass of the continent was much greater. Great areas of land that are now under the sea were once the homelands of Aboriginal groups. In the oral-records of people living on the sea coast to the north, north-east and north-west of the continent, there exist stories of places, now under the sea, which were once important ritual performance centres and which remain important sources of spiritual power.

Thousands of years ago the climate and, consequently, the condition of the land in many parts of Australia was very different. Archaeological evidence from the Willandra Lakes region in south-west New South Wales shows that the lakes were once a flourishing centre of life. Thirty-five thousand years ago, people lived on the birds and fish of the lakes and the abundant plant and animal food sources found in the fertile land fed by the rivers. It is hard to imagine this abundance in the arid, barren landscape of the region today. It is equally difficult to imagine people living in an Australia where volcanoes were active, as they once were in western Victoria, and where giant kangaroos, echidnas, koalas and diprotodons roamed grassy plains and lush, tropical jungles.

Yet Aboriginal people were part of these times and, as the archaeological evidence shows, even in these early years they had mastery of the land. They developed social organisations, adapted and refined

11 Australia at the time of low sea level during the Ice Age (CA)

12 Skeleton of a 3000-year-old dingo excavated at Fromm's Landing, South Australia (D.T. Mulvaney)

13 Early evidence of rock art, Koonalda Cave, South Australia (R. Edwards)

14 Lake Mungo, New South Wales. Archeaologists have found tools here which are over 30 000 years old (AOIS)

11

4

technology, controlled plant growth, husbanded scarce resources and evolved a highly complex religious explanation for the relationships not only between themselves but also between themselves and their lands.

Knowledge about Australia's ancient history has been gathered from the excavation and analysis of archaeological sites all over mainland Australia and Tasmania.

To get a picture of Aboriginal lifestyles before 1788, information, apart from archaeological evidence, can be gained from ethnographic accounts contained in the writings of the early European settlers and the scientific research of the 19th Century and 20th Century ethnographers.

Ethnographic evidence shows that there were once 600 to 700 political units in Australia. These units shared a common language or dialect. Families sharing descent from a common ancestor formed clans which came together from time to time to conduct important religious ceremonies, to trade, to arrange marriages and to settle inter-clan disputes. Mostly, though, people stayed together in their 'core' family groups (that is, husband, wife and their children) with, perhaps, some close friends to share the responsibilities of normal daily routines. Sometimes several 'core' families and their friends formed a larger domestic group. Decisions were arrived at through discussion, with the opinions of the more senior members of the group, especially those with recognised expertise in the issues under debate, carrying the most weight. The ways in which Aborigines once lived, particularly prior to 1788, indicate that they followed a structured social and political system that allowed them to manage both themselves and their lands to maximum mutual advantage.

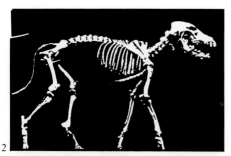

12

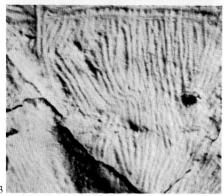

13

14

Australia Bound (1400-1788)

When the first overseas visitors came to Australia is not known. Certainly contact with people of Papua New Guinea goes back thousands of years and, in some Aboriginal oral traditions, there are stories of people who came from the sea. These were the mysterious Baiini who entered the mythical tradition of Aboriginal people in Australia's north.

There is historical evidence to show that a number of visitors began to hover around the Australian coast and even came ashore briefly from the 15th Century on.

There is some reason to believe the great Chinese admiral of the Ming Dynasty (1368–1644), Cheng Ho was the earliest of the explorers to visit Australia. He made seven great voyages of discovery between 1405 and 1432, visiting regions bordering the Indian Ocean including East Africa, India, Java and Sumatra. He may have also landed near where Darwin now stands in 1432. A Chinese statuette found in Darwin in 1879 and some porcelain found in the Gulf of Carpentaria support this theory but the evidence is not conclusive.

For a period of 200 years to just after the end of the 19th Century, at least 1000 Macassans came south each year in their fishing *praus* from the Indonesian island of Sulewesi. They came to the Arnhem Land and Kimberley coasts to fish for the sea slug *trepang* or *beche-de-mer*. Their visits are well documented in Aboriginal art and stories and some of their words have been preserved in a few Aboriginal languages. Also their presence is evidenced in the technology and plants they introduced and in archaeological sites in northern Australia. Some Aboriginal families today have Macassan ancestors and relations. As regular visitors they were generally welcomed by Aborigines who sometimes travelled back with them to Macassar. However, the Australian Government finally put a stop to these visits in 1907 because of their threat to English pearling interests.

In the 16th and 17th centuries the Portuguese and Spanish navigators pioneered the trans-Pacific sea routes. A Spanish attempt to colonise the Great South Land went awry when the land they proclaimed in 1606 as 'Australia del Espiritu Santo' proved to be an island in today's Vanuatu. The commander, Pedro Fernandez de Quiros, tried to return with a second expedition in 1615 but with his death on route, the Spanish interest in Australia died. In 1606 Quiros' deputy, Luis Vaez de Torres, sailed through the strait that bears his name. The Spanish crews captured a number of Islanders to take back to Spain but it is not certain whether they arrived — all that is known is that they reached the Philippines. The first known European paintings of Torres Strait Islanders were made by Torres' deputy commander, Diego Prado de Tovar, on this voyage in 1606.

The Dutch also explored the northern, western and southern Australian coast from 1606. What they saw did not impress them and, though they left some names on the Australian map, they made no claim to any of the territory. Their initial encounters with Aborigines quickly dissuaded them from exploring further portions of the land. Willem de Vlamingh in 1697 ordered 'sixteen cautious land surveys' on the western coast but when confronted by Aborigines withdrew. The Dutch found the original Australians, on the whole, fierce and warlike.

Despite the English pirate William Dampier's negative reports in 1688 about the land and the people, the English had their eyes fixed on territory in the Pacific. Captain James Cook was instructed to take possession of the eastern half of the continent for the British Crown. This Cook duly did when he sailed up the fertile east coast of the continent. At Possession Island, off Cape York Peninsula, he took possession of the whole of the eastern coast in the name of King George III. Neither Cook nor the botanist Joseph Banks took much notice of the people who already inhabited the land. They were quite ready to declare that the country was unoccupied and unowned (*terra nullius*) and was therefore quite open to colonisation.

15

15 Macassan prau (A. Roberts)

16 Spanish watercolour of Torres Strait Islanders painted by Diego Prado de Tovar in 1606 (reproduced from *Terra Australis: the Furthest Shore* by William Eisler and Bernard Smith, International Cultural corporation of Australia, Sydney, 1988)

17 The First Fleet in Botany Bay from the *Illustrated Sydney News*, March 1871 (NLA)

16

17

Invasion—1788

18 January 1788 marked the beginning of an abrupt change in the human history of the Australian continent. On this day the first of a fleet of ships from England sailed into Botany Bay. Some days later the assembled fleet sailed a few miles north of Botany Bay and anchored in a great harbour which they later called Port Jackson. From the ships came convict men and women, marine guards and the officers sent to govern them. On 26 January 1788 a flag was hoisted and, with speeches, proclamations and the firing of muskets, a new British colony was established.

Eora clan lands in 1788 bordered those parts of the harbour where the invasion began. The Eora must surely have been amazed at the large number of strange looking people who had arrived in their land and who instantly set about destroying it—chopping down the trees, clearing scrub,

pitching tents, making paths to freshwater, unpacking stores and so on. It was not long before conflict developed between the Eora people and English officers and convicts. As the newcomers began helping themselves to Eora food resources and their possessions (such as spears, baskets and fish nets) and began interfering with their women, confrontation was inevitable. In March and May 1788 the Eora were reported as having speared various convicts and by November of the same year Governor Phillip said that race relations were not improving: Aborigines 'now avoid us more than they did when we first landed'.

Aborigines from around Botany Bay were especially resentful of the manner by which the British occupied their lands. Cook fired on them when he landed but Phillip's tentative dealings with them on his journeys around the bay were without violence or bloodshed. Nevertheless, resistance grew.

It was two years after settlement when relations between the Aborigines around Sydney and the British broke down completely. On 10 December 1790, the first of a succession of courageous Aboriginal guerilla leaders was noted in dispatches. His name was Pemulwuy and when on this day he speared the Governor's gamekeeper, John McIntire, in retaliation for dreadful crimes against the Eora, twelve years of guerilla warfare commenced. With guerilla bands Pemulwuy fought against the New South Wales Corps until he was killed by two bounty hunters in 1802.

The Dharuk people from the Cumberland Plains area beyond Parramatta also took to fighting for their lands. A battle took place between them and members of the New South Wales Corps on Richmond Hill (what is now known as the Hawkesbury near north Richmond) in June 1795. From 1788 to 1830 the Eora, the Dharuk and other coastal people to the north and south of Sydney found their lands taken from them, their bravest warriors and hunters killed, and their families decimated by murder and disease. Only small pockets of people were left to survive in their own country.

Dispossession and what turned out to be almost genocide, marked the pattern of occupation of Aboriginal lands for the next hundred years and this pattern was established in the first few decades after the arrival of the First Fleet. Until the end of the 19th Century, Aboriginal people throughout the continent resisted the occupation of their lands by the British. Names of great resistance leaders such as Pemulwuy, Brian Boru, Musquito, Dundalli, Pigeon are well known but many others whose exploits were never recorded are sadly forgotten now. Battles were dismissed by the British. Their reports referred only to the 'dispersing of natives', 'rounding up of treacherous savages', 'the murder of peaceful settlers'. Seldom did either official dispatches or

news reports acknowledge that a state of war existed. Today, however, historians are piecing together a history of Aboriginal people resisting white settlement and fighting for their lands.

In turn, each area of white settlement became a battlefield and, in the three eastern States, para-military forces such as the dreaded Native Mounted Police were established to combat Aboriginal guerilla tactics. The last recorded pitched battle in defence of the country was fought in 1884 at the site of Battle Mountain (between Mount Isa and Cloncurry in north Queensland) when the Kalkadoons fought the Queensland Native Mounted Police and a group of pastoralists. One of the last massacres was at Coniston in the Northern Territory in 1928.

The enumeration of Aborigines in Australian censuses has always been complicated and error prone. However, it has been recorded that within a century of the coming of the British, from a population of almost a million, fewer than 50 000 Aboriginal people remained. The total for all the Australian States in 1901 was 48 248

19

20

20 Aboriginal rock painting depicting a massacre, Innesvale, Northern Territory
(R. Edwards)

18 Battle sites in the Sydney region in the 1790s (AII)
19 Guerilla attack on a shepherd's hut, Port Lincoln, South Australia, 1864 (NLA)

9

(Smith 1980:12) and while this is not an accurate figure, it was the official estimate at that time.

From the 1870s, many Aborigines were rounded up into mission and government reserves 'for their own protection'. Misguided Europeans sought to protect Aborigines from disease, neglect and moral depravity. Until as late as the 1960s children, especially those who were only partly of Aboriginal descent, were forcibly taken from their Aboriginal mothers. This was in an attempt to deny them their Aboriginality and to assimilate them into Euro-Australian society.

21

23

22

21 Chained Aboriginal prisoners, Western Australia (NLA)

22 Tasmanian Aborigines, Oyster Cove, Tasmania in the 1860s (NLA)

23 Aboriginal State ward in domestic service (AIAS)

24 The Rainbow Serpent carved deep rivers (AOIS)

25 A person's Dreaming comes from the land (AOIS)

People and Land

Today it is recognised that Australia was not *terra nullius,* a land without people, before European settlement. However, it was considered *terra nullius* in 1788 when the First Fleet arrived. This meant in English law that the new continent was without a recognisable system of government, and without any form of commerce or evidence of land ownership. Although Aboriginal people inhabited the land, the British considered that, under the terms of *terra nullius*, they were entitled to occupy it as they were the first to claim it. Not even a treaty was required since there was no recognisable government with which to negotiate. Trade agreements could not be entered into since no goods were produced for trade, and land could not be purchased or conquered since there were no owners to sell or defend it.

24

25

Captain James Cook did not hesitate to claim half the continent of Australia on the basis of *terra nullius* for the English after his 1769 voyage up the east cost.

Many years were to pass before the true nature of government, land ownership and land use in Aboriginal Australia became known to white Australians. Europeans are only now understanding that Aboriginal land ownership is based on religious beliefs and ties.

As in the past, Aboriginal clans today hold deep religious links with their lands which were formed in the Dreamtime. The land belongs to the Aborigines and the Aborigines to the land. They are bound in everlasting union. The great ancestral creative beings, who journeyed across the continent at the beginning of time, established the land boundaries between different Aboriginal groups and the sacred sites. Carrying out ritual obligations at these sacred sites and performing religious cere-

monies are the ways by which Aborigines feel bound to their lands and protective towards it.

In the heroic sagas of the Dreamtime the ancestral creative beings roamed the country carving the valleys, making the rivers flow and raising the mountains. They left behind mysterious caverns, sculptured rock formations and cliffs and then they filled the tree-draped, shady pools with their own spirit-children. Finally, they filled the land that they had created with living things drawn from themselves such as plants and animals, fishes, birds and people.

Totems represent the link between Aborigines and the ancestral creative beings. The kangaroo, for instance, is a manifestation of the Kangaroo ancestral being, the barramundi the Baramundi ancestor. Himans get their spiritual identification from these totems at birth or just before they are born. Just before a mother becomes aware of her baby she or her husband is given a sign— perhaps in a dream, or in a strange experience or a trance-like vision — that a spirit child has entered her womb. A magpie may fly into the path of the mother while she is out walking. This may be the sign that she is pregnant so, when the baby is born, he or she is spiritually linked to the Magpie ancestral being and the child belongs to that Magpie Dreaming or totem. A person in this way may be linked to a kangaroo, a barramundi, a plant or something in the heavens. Aborigines, therefore, are directly linked to an ancestral being via that being's appearance in their subconscious or by its physical manifestation in the landscape. It is a spiritual link and is sometimes called a person's Dreaming.

Aboriginal people are bound to their land by these spiritual links. Away from their own lands they are endangered by spiritual forces whose powers they can neither assess nor control. Even within their own lands there are places where they are in spiritual danger. These are places not open to them (because they have not been initiated into their mysteries) or places they fail to approach with due respect. By contrast, there are places in their own land to which particular Aborigines are tied by personal spiritual links and these are places to which their spirit will return when they die. These are safe places for them.

Each clan's land is dotted with sites of spiritual significance. Clans and particular individuals have responsibility for these places. They have to see that they are cared for, kept free from unauthorised visitors and are served by proper ritual performances when these fall due. These performances bring back the ancestral being's presence and, by performing them, Aborigines show respect for the ancestral beings' powers which, when released, renew the land and all life in it.

26

27

28

26 Kangaroos are part of some Aborigines Dreaming (AOIS)

27. 28 Totemic figures featured in rock art (AOIS)

29 Ritual estate, the Olgas (AOIS)

30 Women dancing in a public ceremony, Utopia, Northern Territory (AOIS)

Living with the Land

The sites of spiritual significance or 'sacred sites' as they tend to be called now, form part of the 'ritual estate' of each Aboriginal clan. Those responsible for a sacred site are accountable to the whole clan for the way in which they carry out their ritual tasks. Any negligence can cause great harm to their people, for instance, food and water supplies may run short, natural disasters may overwhelm them or a mysterious illness may afflict the group. Punishments, laid down in the Dreamtime, are harsh for those who neglect their spiritual responsibilities.

Caring for the land does not rely entirely on the performance of ritual. Ritual releases the spiritual power necessary to make the estate and all things in it fertile but long experience has taught the Aboriginal people that the power of the spirit is helped by certain actions. Setting fire to the land, for instance, encourages new growth which attracts animals and birds to feed on the fresh food, and careful husbanding of animal and food supplies allows for a basic stock to be left which regenerates in the new season. Replanting of the root-top and vine ensured the re-growth of many edible root plants.

Prior to 1788 Aboriginal people lived in comparative affluence. Certainly those whose lands bordered the sea, or lay in riverine valleys or at the edges of lakes, had ready access to a variety of foods. For these Aborigines in fertile areas the daily task of fishing, hunting and gathering food took no more than two to three hours. In Victoria, so successful were people near the rivers and lakes in ensuring a regular supply of food with a minimum of effort that they established permanent stone settlements. In other places, people moved around their lands to take advantage of the seasonal foods and to vary their diet. They also wanted to husband the land, to carry out ritual and to visit places which had special meaning for them. Aborigines did not wander aimlessly, desperately searching for food and drink in a daily struggle for survival. This is still a common misconception.

29

30

13

As in the past, groups of Aborigines today try to remain close to their own lands. They do so not only because of the spiritual links that tie them but also because they have special knowledge of their own lands which guarantee their ability to survive. Only in conditions of extreme scarcity do groups cross into neighbouring lands, and then only after diplomatic negotiations with the lands' custodians regarding the use of resources. Places of ritual significance are avoided and any gathered food is shared with the host group. People living in barren country with little water might need to seek help from their neighbours from time to time but, in normal times, the land over which groups range to hunt and gather their seasonal foods is their own.

The major landowning group in Australia is commonly called the 'tribe' although the term is inaccurate. The concept of the 'tribe' has never applied to Aborigines since it implies a form of political organisation that has never existed in Aboriginal society. Nonetheless, the term has continued into popular usage.

In the early 1970s the ethnographer, Norman Tindale, produced an historical 'tribal' map showing over 600 landowning groups before white settlement. It is no longer possible to estimate with any accuracy the size of these groups. The size of the area of land they occupied is not in itself any indication of the size of each group. Some groups like the Wiradjuri and Kamilaroi 'tribes' in New South Wales occupied large land areas and it is known from historic reports that they formed large nations of people. This was because their lands were generally well watered and fertile. Pintubi people in the north-central desert regions of Australia owned an equally large area of land but it could support only a comparatively small population. The Irukandji people who occupied the coastal strip and rainforest areas to the north of Cairns in Queensland were probably more numerous than the Pintubi, though living in a land area only a fraction of the size of the Pintubi land. Their land was well watered and rich in its variety of plant and animal life and was capable of supporting many more people than similar areas of land elsewhere in Australia.

Climatic and environmental conditions were, in the main, what determined the size of each group's land and the number of people it should support. Aborigines knew how important it was to control their populations. Each group's land could sustain only so many people. Skilful management of the available resources did in some cases increase food supplies which allowed a growth in the population.

The evidence now being gathered seems to indicate that in the 500 years or so prior to 1788, there was an intensification of the use of food resources in some parts of the country. This was the result of applying regeneration techniques to the land, improving hunting skills and using a wider range of resources. This same period also saw an increase in social and trading interaction between groups and some changes in social organisation.

The basic social unit in Aboriginal society is the family. Small groups of families reside together and form a 'band'. The size of a 'band' varies considerably depending mainly on the availability of food. A 'band' then is a number of families who live and hunt together.

In a 'band' there are different 'clans'. A 'clan' means that all its members are descended from a common ancestor. They could be descended from the Possum ancestor or Kangaroo ancestor or any other ancestral being. People cannot marry members of the same clan. Because 'bands' comprise married people with families their members represent a number of different clans. This means that in a band you may

31

31 Section from the Tindale Tribal Map (AOIS)
32, 33, 34 Firemaking in Central Australia
(R. Edwards)

find Possum people married to Kangaroo people, or Magpie people married to Snake people. A 'band' is a residential group whereas a 'clan' is a descent group.

'Clan' members share the responsibility for looking after their ritual estate and it is the 'clan' that constitutes the major political unit in Aboriginal society. The clan comes together only to share in seasonally abundant resources, to carry out ceremonial rituals, arrange marriages and to settle inter-clan disputes. A number of clans will meet together for major ceremonies.

Fire Making

Fire is usually made by friction created with a fire-drill or fire-saw. To use a fire-drill a pit is made in a softwood stick, or sometimes a shield. A thin hardwood 'drill' is rapidly twirled between the palms of the hands as they are moved up and down the drill-stick. This action produces a smouldering wood powder which is tipped on to tinder, blown gently and swung into the air. Ignition takes about a minute.

The other friction method of making fire is by means of a 'fire-saw'. The edge of a hardwood stick is drawn rapidly to and fro across a cleft stick containing tinder. In Central Australia a hardwood spear-thrower is rubbed across a soft-wood shield to produce the smouldering wood powder.

Fire is sometimes made by striking a piece of flint held on a pad of timber with a piece of ironstone or iron pyrites. The sparks drop onto tinder and ignite.

Dried grass, finely shredded bark, dead leaves, bird feathers, animal hair and fur, are used as tinder in fire making.

Fire is made to a pre-judged level of heat. Hardwoods are selected to generate hot coals for efficient cooking; a low flame can be produced when heat is required to soften gum which is got from spinifex or other plants and used to mount stone tools on handles or the ends of spear-throwers. These gums are thermo-plastics, softening upon heating to a low temperature and becoming extremely hard when cold. Dried leaves and light brush is used to provide brilliant illumination during evening ceremonies.

32

33

34

15

Family Life

Even today one of the most notable characteristics of Aboriginal and Islander people is the strength of their family ties and their awareness of family obligations. Australians who are not themselves Aborigines will find their Aboriginal friends making them 'family' and giving them a position in the family. This process of classifying people who are not related as members of the family is an ancient tradition in Aboriginal society. It is only when strangers have established their real or classificatory relationship with each other that they know how to behave with each other — how they should speak to each other, what respect is due and what obligations are required. Obligations are determined by one person's relationship to the other, just as they are with members of any family.

Aboriginal systems of kinship can be made to seem very complex to the outsider. Aboriginal children learn their own family system by living with the family unit and learning how they are related to each of the other members. In doing so they learn how they may address each family member and what their responsibility is to each one, just as they learn their own rights and what respect they are due. Children learn their relationships to both sides of their family. Among the more important relatives are their mother's sisters whom they also call 'mother' and their father's brothers whom they also call 'father'. For boys, their mother's brother is very important since usually he will be responsible for their initiation .

Mother's brothers and others who stand in this 'exogomous' relationship to the children are also important because they will be the parents of the children's potential marriage partners. Because of this, children learn to show great respect to their future mothers-in-law and fathers-in-law. Boys, especially, avoid looking at or speaking to women whose daughters they might marry. The kinship law requires that children should marry out of their own line of descent.

Not all of today's Aborigines follow the strict traditions of kinship and marriage, though many do. Women who would normally be expected to marry the person chosen for them are now, sometimes, wanting to make their own choice from the range of partners who are suitable for them. In urban and country communities where traditional practices are no longer fully observed, marriages are left to individual choice.

35

36

35 Alan Maratja Dhamarrandji and his family on Galiwin'ku (Elcho Island) (AII)

36 Gathering yams for food (State Library of South Australia)

16

Daily Life

Because in the past Aborigines were hunters and gatherers it was important to share out responsibilities efficiently so that each person could share effectively and productively in the life of the group. Women and men accepted different responsibilities, in part determined by the woman's child-bearing role. Men were the tool-makers, the hunters and the custodians of male ritual and law. Women bore and reared the children, gathered the steady staple food supply of small animals, plants and insects, prepared it and shared it out. When men were successful in the hunt, the meat was an important addition to the diet. Women also had responsibility for their own law and rituals and taught their knowledge to the younger women and girls.

Apart from this normal division of responsibilities between men and women, there was some specialisation in Aboriginal society. Some people were, for instance, more skilful at searching out food, or painting and weaving, or perhaps playing a musical instrument.

When men went out to hunt animals — to spear fish, to trap birds or to run down the large reptiles — it was important that all members of the party knew what to do. For instance, they had to be able to recognise the distinct marks left by different animals, be able to tell how recently the marks had

been made and in which direction the animals had gone. Once an animal had been successfully tracked down, each of the hunters had to know what his role was in the actual capture of the prey. Sometimes a single hunter was lucky and he would catch a goanna or an emu on his own, but usually hunters worked as a team and shared the game they caught.

Women, too, usually went out in groups to dig up root plants, gather water-lily bulbs, collect seed for milling or to pick fruit. Together they might also catch any small animals or reptiles that they saw. There was a fairly wide choice of food available, although it varied according to climate and environment. A recent study

37 Fishing with scoop nets (Australian Museum)
38 Collecting onion tree orchids (AOIS)
39 Carrying water (H. Basedow)

by Isaacs (1987) listed around 230 plant species from all over Australia that were used as food by Aborigines and Torres Strait Islanders. Many of them still are.

Children usually accompanied the women when they went to collect food. Adolescent girls were expected to work closely with the women so that they could learn to recognise and harvest food crops, but the younger children were left free to play. Their playing, however, usually involved looking for fruit so learning to identify edible fruits and nuts, and knowing when to pick them, came quickly to small children.

Nature itself informed Aborigines of the presence of seasonal fruits. The call of a particular bird announced that a seasonal fruit was ripening. The flowering of certain trees signalled that crabs were ready for eating or that oysters were available. In a time when Aborigines relied more heavily on bush tucker they looked carefully for these sorts of signs. Such signs would tell them not only where to make camp but also where exactly a seasonal food could be found in abundance.

Not all foods were immediately ready for eating. Some plants in their untreated state were poisonous. Others needed to have their bitterness or excessive acidity tempered with other blander flavours. Flesh of an animal or a fish was rarely eaten raw.

A variety of styles of cooking, including baking, steaming and boiling were used. Plant foods were also prepared in a variety of ways. Some foods needed to be mashed and leached in water before they could be cooked and eaten. Seed had to be ground and the flour mixed with water and roasted before eating. Sometimes the flour was mixed in with other vegetables and meats and cooked in a bark wrapping.

Food was distributed among the members of each core family according to established rules of precedence and need. Besides the rules for wise management and conservation of resources, there were rules about who could eat certain foods, how much they could eat and when it should be eaten. Tasmanians over the recent millenia, for instance, made fish taboo to everyone, though it had originally been an important part of their diet. At initiation ceremonies, young boys generally had to avoid eating certain types of meat. Such rules were not universal. Each group had its own rules about how food should be shared and when it should and should not be eaten by certain people.

42

44

43

Knowledge about bush food has been handed down through the generations and is carefully preserved by many of today's Aboriginal and Torres Strait Island people even though 'bush tucker' does not feature regularly in their diets. Aborigines and Islanders now have access to readily available foods on supermarket shelves. Nonetheless, people living in the country or by the sea will have special knowledge of the places where particularly good native foods are found and they know a variety of ways for collecting and preparing them for eating.

40 Fish traps on the Darling River. New South Wales (C. Kerry)

41 Returning from a successful hunt (AOIS)

42 Muttonbirding in Tasmania (AOIS)

43 Cooking bush turkey, Utopia, Northern Territory (AOIS)

44 Shopping in a supermarket (AOIS)

Home and Garden

For many years it was the custom in school texts to emphasise the apparent contrast between lives of Aboriginal and Islander people and that of other Australians. Usually this meant pointing out the things Aborigines and Islanders were thought not to do. School students, even Aboriginal and Islander school students, learnt that Aboriginal and Islander people did not wear clothes, live in houses or work. Such broad generalisations were incorrect. Aborigines did wear garments, they also built permanent dwellings and they certainly worked. These generalisations were based on narrow definitions of clothing, housing and work and, furthermore, they were based on European yardsticks.

Torres Strait Islanders developed economic lifestyles suited to their island environment. On some of the islands with appropriate soils and climate they cultivated crops and bred animals for food. All the independent island communities exploited the resources of the sea. They developed a technology which helped them not only in their sea-faring activities but also in making the best use of their island land. A variety of house styles was favoured ranging from the Murray Island round houses, which were built in clusters and surrounded by permanent fences, to the less elaborate temporary houses erected on those islands where the lack of permanent water prevented long-term occupation.

Aborigines also varied the design of their houses according to climate, availability of materials for construction and the likely period of occupancy. On the west coast of Tasmania, conical houses, thatched with grass and large enough to house as many as thirty people, were gathered in villages of up to seventeen houses. These served as dwellings for approximately six months. Aborigines in Victoria, as well as developing clever techniques for ensuring a regular supply of food through an ingenious system of canals and storage dams by the Murray River, built permanent stone houses. In Cape York and Arnhem Land, housing was designed to allow people the maximum comfort in the wet season when the condition of the rivers and swamp land

45 Traditional housing, MacDonnell Range, Central Australia (South Australia Museum Collection)

46 Stringybark hut on stilts (AOIS)

47 Outstation housing, Docker River, Northern Territory (AOIS)

48 Aboriginal housing at Yulara, near Uluru (AOIS)

45

20

made travel almost impossible. In the hot desert areas weatherproof shelters or *wiltjas* were constructed with arched boughs set firmly into the ground in an oval and secured at the apex. Spinifex, brush or leafy boughs were used to cover the framework.

It was not the custom for Aborigines and Islanders to enclose with walls all the functional areas of their homes. Space was allocated outside the main living area for meeting visitors, both male and female. Food preparation and cooking was done in a special cooking area while tool-making and repairs were carried out by a fire in another space. Living, for the most part, was done in the open where band members could see other members going about their daily business.

Today, in many parts of Australia, there are Aboriginal and Islander people who still prefer to live outside their homes as much as possible. Housing designed for Aboriginal people in those remote parts of Australia where traditional practices are followed often attempt to meet the criteria of customary use.

Variety in house styles was also reflected in the range of designs in household equipment. Three important implements in catching and gathering food were the spear, the throwing stick and the digging stick. Spear designs were determined by their purpose and by the materials available for their construction. Spears were used to kill animals, birds and reptiles as well as fish. They were also used as weapons in war and as ceremonial objects in clan rituals. Some spears were made of heavy wood, some of lighter wood, some of reed or bamboo. Some were made of one piece with the point and shaft carefully shaped and the point hardened in fire. Others had a joint at which the head was bound to the shaft. The head was made of wood, bone, stone or fish spines, and was barbed, single, double or triple-pronged. Each spear was sharpened and shaped according to its specific use. Every hunter had a number of spears and the one he selected depended on the kind of animal he wanted to hunt. Ceremonial spears were elaborately carved, painted and ornamented, and greatly treasured. There were many regional variations in design.

47

46

48

21

Spears in Australia are usually associated with the spear-thrower or *woomera* (from the Dharuk language of Sydney). This was used both in parts of New South Wales and the Northern Territory and served as a multiple use implement. It was principally a tool to increase the force and extend the range of the spear throw. A short stone blade attached to the throwing end allowed it to be used as an adze. Some *woomeras*, which were of a narrow design and made of hardwood, were occasionally used for making fire by sawing across a piece of dry softwood. Elongated bowl-shaped ones were used as carrying dishes.

In the National Museum Collection in Victoria there are many delicately carved and painted spear-throwers on display. These were collected in the 19th Century from Victoria, South Australia and southern New South Wales.

Throwing sticks, which were tucked into human hair waist-belts worn by hunters, were an important part of the hunter's weaponry. Used skilfully they could stun or kill animals and reptiles and frighten birds into catching nets. *Boomerangs* (a word which also comes from the Dharuk language) were used for much the same function. One type of boomerang, that if it failed to hit its mark, was designed to return to the thrower.

Digging sticks were generally used by women. These too were multi-purpose implements which could serve a variety of functions. They were rarely carefully shaped or decorated because of their purely utilitarian use. At one end they were pointed. They were made of solid wood and there was very little variation in their design. Today they are sometimes replaced by steel crowbars which are used for digging out rabbit warrens.

49 Grinding grass seeds, Central Australia (National Museum of Victoria Collection)

50 Stone-tipped spear, Cape York, Queensland (AOIS)

51 Skin cloaks were worn in the south (South Australia Museum Collection)

· 52 Shaping a spear-thrower (South Australia Museum Collection)

50

49

51

The Boomerang

Originally, boomerang *just meant throwing stick. The hunter normally did not require a throwing stick to return. Its purpose was to hit and injure its target sufficiently to enable it to be captured, or slow enough for the spear throwers to get into range. Over time, and in different regions, intricate designs were elaborated which allowed throwing sticks to curve around obstructions, to skip with force off the ground, to catch on to and swing around a protective shield and to swirl in a large arc eventually to curve back to the thrower.*

The returning boomerang *is limited to games, killing birds and directing animals into traps. Light and thin, with a deep curvature in relation to length, the ends are slightly twisted in opposite directions while the lower surface is flat and the upper surface convex.*

The most widely used non-returning boomerang *is the Central Australian type. Made from a carefully selected curved limb of a mulga tree it has fluting on the upper surface and a flat underside neatly finished with adze marks. These* boomerangs *have a coating of red ochre, and when used in ceremonies may be painted with decorative white, yellow and black designs.*

The boomerang *has a multiplicity of uses. Besides its function as a fighting or hunting weapon it serves to clear grass and soil to prepare comfortable campsites or ceremonial grounds; it is used as a poker and shovel when cooking, the ashes being scraped away to make room for a carcase and the cooked food also being raked out from the ashes. The sharp end of a hardwood* boomerang *is sometimes employed for cutting up a cooked animal or for digging holes for an earth oven or the erection of ceremonial regalia; outcrops of stone are dug out with* boomerangs *to get unweathered material for implements; the sharp edge can be used to create friction in firemaking; two of these weapons tapped together are sometimes an accompaniment to ceremonies, the rapid vibrating sound only being properly made by experts. Other* boomerangs *serve as sacred objects.*

52

53 Bringing wood into camp
(H. Basedow)
54 Men with fighting weapons
(H. Basedow)

53

54

23

Transport

Traditionally, Aborigines never travelled at speed. Hunting and foraging excursions were planned in advance and travelling time was always allowed for. Similarly, seasonal journeys to new crops, to favoured camps or to ceremonial gatherings were timed to allow for the distance to be covered at a comfortable pace. Journeys like these usually took a day or so.

The only Aborigines who travelled great distances at comparative speed were the messengers. These young men, carrying marked message sticks to help them recall and authenticate their messages, were sent out to neighbouring bands to invite them to attend important ceremonies or meetings. Like all travellers these messengers were careful to take defined safe routes — that is, routes that took them away from spiritually dangerous sites and that showed them to be travellers passing through the country on legitimate business. On reaching an encampment a messenger waited at a distance but in view of the camp residents until a senior person came out to meet him. This senior person then established the messenger's identity, inspected his credentials in the form of the message stick, assigned him a family relationship and, finally, invited him to come to sit in the guest place near the appropriate host person. Every courtesy was shown to the messenger who observed the proper protocol. His host was the person who was thought to be in a proper relationship to him and whose location in the camp put the guest closest to his own lands.

Aborigines crossed water only when it was not possible to walk around it. When it was necessary to take to rivers and lakes in order to fish, a variety of boat materials and boat designs were used. Makeshift rafts of logs bound together were used to cross rivers. On the lakes of the lower Murray River women used rafts constructed from layers of reeds to reach mussel beds far from the shore. Eight to ten women occupied one raft which was propelled with a single pole. The women dived from the rafts in search of shellfish and crayfish. Afterwards the caught food was cooked on the rafts over fires built on platforms of wet sea-weed and sand.

The simplest form of canoe was the bark canoe which was made from a single sheet of thick bark. This vessel was found in the protected inland waters of the Murray–Darling Basin in western Victoria and in the south-east of South Australia. The ends were pointed and the bark was manipulated while still fresh and pliable to form a boat which was used for crossing rivers and lakes and for fishing. They were usually propelled by punting a long pole.

On the rivers and creeks of coastal New South Wales and in south-east Victoria a second type of canoe was used. These canoes were made from large cylindrical sheets of bark which were turned inside-out and bound at the ends with fibre rope. The outer bark shell of the canoe was straightened by rod-shaped stretchers fixed across the canoe and pliant branches forced into the body to act as ribs.

Boats, dug out of tree trunks, in the style of craft introduced by the Macassans, were used until recent times in north Australia. On the tropical northern and Queensland coasts not only was the dug-out canoe used but also the sewn bark canoe. Normally this was used for longer periods at sea or journeys down rivers. The sewn canoe was constructed from broad strips of bark stitched together and strengthened with a network of ties, stretchers, braces and ribs. Poles were lashed along the bulwarks to act as gunwales and to prevent the sides from collapsing.

Aborigines travelled long distances over sea channels to islands around the Australian coasts. They could do so only in calm conditions as their boats were scarcely adequate. If the distance was too great to an island destination, Aboriginal communities living on those islands might be isolated for long periods. Alternatively such islands might be left uninhabited or visited only rarely to obtain valuable food supplies or to carry out ritual at important religious sites. Although knowledge about technologically advanced seacraft was available to them for hundreds if not thousands of years, in general Aborigines did not make use of this knowledge, except in some parts of Arnhem Land. This was probably because they deemed the craft available to them as adequate for their purposes.

Torres Strait Islanders shared seafaring skills with the Papua New Guineans and designed boats with sails, outriggers and for a number of paddles. Being so reliant on the sea for so much of their food and manufacturing materials, as well as for trade and social meetings, they needed advanced water transport that could carry them long distances, in large numbers, and with safety in a variety of weather conditions.

56

55 Types of watercraft
(J.R.B. Love)

56 Modern transport
(All)

57 Canoe tree, Blanchetown, South Australia (R. Edwards)

55

57

25

Trade and Exchange

Trade routes crisscrossed Australia from Cape York south to the South Australian coast, north-west to the Kimberleys and the Daley River and south again to Perth. Goods were sent along these routes and included such articles as shell, wood, gums, ochre and a variety of manufactured items such as tools, ornaments and sacred objects. These items as well as songs and dances were exchanged at 'trade fairs' which occurred at intervals along well-known trade routes. At these fairs, neighbouring groups met, food was plentiful and goods were exchanged or traded. Sometimes marriages were arranged and legal disputes settled. Trade and gift exchange were important aspects of Aboriginal economic, social and ritual life.

Small sections of bailer shells, chipped and ground into oval-shaped pieces, were sent on the trade route from Cape York to southern Australia. These items were ascribed great significance and were used in sorcery and sacred rituals. The north-south route took in the interior of eastern Australia to Cooper Creek, Lake Eyre and the grindstone quarries in the Flinders Ranges. It continued on to Port Augusta, down Spencer and St Vincent gulfs, through Lake

Alexandrina and the Cooroong and finally reached the mouth of the Glenelg River in western Victoria.

Another important trade route began on the north-west coast of Western Australia and ended near Kalgoorlie. On this route pearl shells, shaped into pendants and often incised on the inner side with patterns, were traded in many parts of the interior. Pearl pendant fragments have been found over 1500 kilometres from their place of origin.

Different types of stone found their way to regions where good quality material was in short supply. Axe-heads from an extensive quarry at Mount William in Victoria reached South Australia and New South Wales. Other axe-heads from quarries in Queensland were traded down river systems to Lake Eyre and Central Australia.

Boomerangs made in Central Australia and the Northern Territory were traded extensively. People in Arnhem Land acquired them for use as musical clap-sticks. The narcotic called *pitcheri* (*Duboisia*

58

59

hopwoodii) which was ground into fragments, mixed with ashes and then chewed
was bartered in special bags.

It was not uncommon for Aboriginal
groups to travel for a few days, on defined
safe tracks across neighbouring lands, in
order to attend trade fairs. Occasionally, so
as to obtain something of very special value
or quality, Aborigines were prepared to
travel great distances. For instance, ochre,
which was highly prized, was available
from only a limited number of deposits.
However, Aborigines from western Queensland were prepared to travel all the way to
the Flinders Ranges of South Australia to
select their own ochre from the rich Flinders quarry.

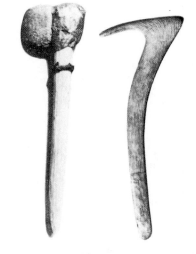

62

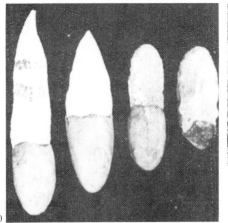

60

63

58 Major trade routes
for pearl and baler
shells (CA)

59 Mat making (AOIS)

60 Quartzite was traded
widely (CA)

61 Quarry for axe
heads, Hopkins River,
Victoria (CA)

62 Stone axes and
boomerangs were
traded (R. Edwards)

63 Ochre pigments for
gift exchange (R. Edwards)

64 Incised pearl shells
(R. Edwards)

61

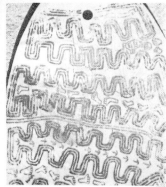

64

27

Healing

As in Western societies there are doctors who diagnose and treat the sick so too in Aboriginal society there are men and women who perform these roles. These are the traditional healers.

Aborigines believe illness and death are caused by sorcerers, spirits or the ancestral creative beings.

If a patient fails to respond to commonly known bush remedies a traditional doctor or healer is consulted. The healer diagnoses the problem and then prescribes some appropriate measures to restore the patient to health. If a patient dies the healer also determines the cause of death.

The traditional healer is usually a person with great spiritual powers. These may have been learnt during an apprenticeship or may have been inherited. It is not uncommon for healers to have strange or visionary experiences. Their special powers allow them to diagnose the cause of illness, cure it, tell the future and protect people against sorcery. Their powers also allow them to travel faster than it would appear humanly possible, anticipate events, know what is happening in faraway places and be able to appear or disappear at will.

In times of illness the healer reassures the patient and patient's family. He or she promotes the correct kind of atmosphere for a sick person to regain faith, confidence and the will to get better. An important part of a healer's function is helping with the patient's psychological welfare. In many ways the role of a healer can be equated with that of a priest, physician and coroner: the priest instils faith, the physician cures the sickness and the coroner determines the cause of misfortune.

Curing minor illnesses may involve just using bush remedies. Most Aboriginal men and women have a knowledge, handed down to them through the generations, of the plants that can be used medicinally. Ailments such as aches and pains, toothache, bites and stings, wounds, boils, constipation and diarrhoea are often treated by the application of plants or minerals known to possess healing qualities. For instance, the fat of the sand goanna soothes burns; ochre made into a paste heals sores; and a solution prepared from the whistling tree (*Casuarina equisetifolia*) is a painkiller for toothaches.

But if a traditional healer is consulted about a serious illness the treatment he or she prescribes is usually of a ritual nature and may include massage, singing and the removal of 'foreign' objects from a patient's body. This type of therapy counteracts the evil powers present in the patient's body. Once the spiritual or supernatural cause of the distress has been removed, the patient starts to get better, both psychologically and physically.

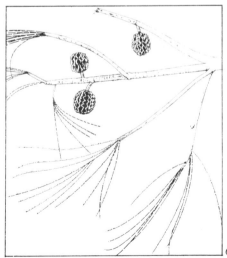

65

Sorcery

Sorcerers are universally feared in Aboriginal Australia as they can cause the illness or death of a victim by projecting an evil spirit or object into the person by 'pointing the bone' or by capturing the person's spirit in a piece of hair or food.

In Central Australia sorcerers wear kurdaitja shoes, made of emu feathers and human blood, to conceal their footprints. Quartz and other crystals, pebbles, pearl shells, australites, many kinds of ornaments and charms are used by sorcerers to cause illness or death.

'Bone pointing' is practised by many groups. Short pieces of bone, pointed at one end and often tipped at the other with a small lump of gum to which is attached a length of human hair string, is used to deadly effect. Sometimes shaped sticks are also used. These are decorated with fine cuts or covered with bird down. Among the Aranda people of Central Australia a man wishing to point the bone first goes away into the bush, places the bone in the ground and repeats curses over it. Later, in the darkness of the night it is pointed secretly at the victim with repeated magical formulae and chants. The person that had been 'boned' sickens and eventually dies unless a traditional healer can discover what is wrong and removes from the body the evil powers responsible.

66

67

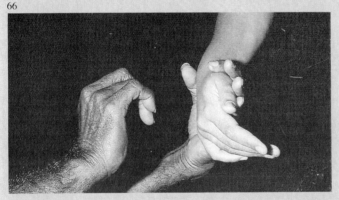

68

69

65 Whistling tree. A solution made from this plant was used to treat toothache
(Reproduced from *Plants and People: Aboriginal Uses of Plants on Groote Eylandt*, Australian Institute of Aboriginal Studies, Canberra, 1981)

66 Healing hands (Neil McLeod)

67 Pointing bones (R. Edwards)

68 Healing rite (National Museum of Victoria Collection)

69 Traditional healer (NLA)

29

Growing up

Aborigines and Islanders have always had a tradition of education. In the past this involved them in learning the skills of living successfully in the natural environment, learning about their religion, and learning about kinship. This included learning the appropriate ways of behaving with family members and understanding their obligations to each other.

In time, if they showed themselves responsible and willing to learn, young Aboriginal men and women would be introduced formally to the full encyclopaedia of spiritual knowledge. They learnt the cycle of songs relating to the acts of creation and were shown the places where the ancestral creative beings performed these great acts. They learnt, too, the dances and became familiar with the paintings, sculptures and the other ritual objects that belonged to each ritual performance cycle. As inheritors of the ritual traditions, young Aboriginal men and women had an obligation to see that those traditions were preserved and that the rituals were performed as required. In time they passed this knowledge and responsibility to their children.

In mastering the range of spiritual knowledge available to them, Aboriginal and Islander men and women gained great prestige in their community. It took thirty to forty years for a person to work through the full series of spiritual initiations. Then, as an initiate, it took many more years for that person to learn the new set of ritual knowledge to which he or she now had access. In view of this long, complicated learning process, men and women who had applied themselves to gaining ritual knowledge were regarded with great respect and were able to take part, with authority, in the councils of the senior members of the community.

This form of ritual education had the purpose of preserving and perpetuating Aboriginal cultural traditions and values. The individual went through learning the spiritual law not only for his or her own personal prestige but also for the benefit of the community and for the children to come.

Today, Aborigines and Islanders in many parts of Australia are still able to learn the law of their own traditions. Those whose ritual education and traditional spiritual practices were disrupted by the coming of the Europeans do not, inevitably, have the same depth of knowledge of spiritual practices as other Aboriginal groups and it is therefore harder for them to sustain their spiritual beliefs. However, although specific knowledge of spiritual practices have in some cases been lost, many of the values taught with the spiritual laws have been retained. It is on these values that Aboriginal and Islander people build their identity.

To ensure that the education their children receive today does not destroy their essential identity, Aborigines and Islanders want to maintain a presence and a voice in schools where their children are taught. Increasingly, education authorities

70

are showing respect for, and placing value on, Aboriginal culture by allowing it to be taught in schools and, as much as possible, by Aborigines and Islanders themselves.

71

72

Games

Boys and girls played games that were largely imitative of adult economic and social life. Boys played with toy weapons and practised at identifying tracks. Small discs of bark were cut from gum trees and bowled along the ground as targets for miniature spears. In regions where boomerangs *were used small models were made and thrown with great skill. Girls played camp games and accompanied their mothers on food collecting expeditions.*

All children learnt songs, dancing, designs and traditional stories; they learnt string games and, like children all over the world, they ran, swam, wrestled, fought and climbed trees.

The Lake Eyre people of South Australia made small round balls from burnt gypsum mixed with water which were spun on a hard surface. The person whose ball spun for the longest time was the winner. A somewhat larger ball, with a small peg fixed in the centre, was used by women playing the same game. Still larger and more solid balls were bowled from opposite sides of a clay pan by two teams of men. The aim was to break up the opponents' balls while they were in motion.

Another game played by men involved throwing a wooden play-stick or wit-wit so that it ricocheted off the hard ground. Many games were contested by opposing sides drawn from different social groups.

70 Children from Galiwin'ku (Elcho Island) (AII)

71 A senior man of the Anbarra people demonstrating the didjeridu (AIAS)

72 Returning from a hunting expedition (AIAS)

73, 74 Children of Nkaria School, Hermannsberg, Central Australia (AII)

73

74

31

Law

Aboriginal laws were encoded in each group's religious tradition. According to that tradition the ancestral creative beings decided, in the Dreamtime when the world began, the rights and responsibilities and the consequent behaviours of all things in the land that they had made. For humans their social organisation, relationships, religious responsibilities to the land and their rights over it were all set out at the time of creation. They were encoded in the stories of that time which were handed down from generation to generation in the dance, music and art of religious ceremony. They were also in the oral tradition passed on by the guardians of that tradition who had gained access to it as initiates.

All Aboriginal and Islander people were familiar with their own laws and with the daily rights and obligations they imposed. From early childhood they learnt what the law allowed and what it forbade. They knew both the spiritual dangers and the punishments that threatened the law breaker, and they witnessed the process by which offences against the law were notified, verified, argued and, finally, decided. The process of law was a process of political negotiation that involved most members of the community. Aborigines made sure that in matters of law not only was justice done but that justice was seen to be done. When there was a dispute, investigations by the senior members of the community were made to discover the seriousness of the offence. Offences regarded as unlawful included unauthorised killing of a person, sacrilege, incest, adultery, theft, unauthorised physical assault, insult and neglect of kinship obligations.

When the guilt and the gravity of the crime were established it was then impor-tant to fix a punishment that the community agreed was appropriate. Punishments could range from making compensation over an agreed period to having to face a squad of spearmen with only a shield and one's agility as protection.

Disputes between Aboriginal groups were settled by negotiation, ritual punishment or formal battles. Settling disputes under Aboriginal law was part of the purpose for the great gatherings of Aboriginal groups that took place periodically. Other purposes were to trade, to exploit an abundant harvest, to arrange marriages and to perform major ceremonies.

The experience of living under two systems of law — the English and Aboriginal — has not been a happy one for all original Australians. In every Australian State and Territory, Aborigines and Islanders have a high rate of imprisonment that is far out of proportion to their numbers in the community.

Today, in many parts of Australia, Aborigines continue to settle offences under their own law. In doing so they frequently find themselves in trouble under Anglo-Australian law. For example: an Aborigine who speared an Aboriginal woman was acting in accordance with 'tribal law' because she had insulted him by gestures and words. However, he was prosecuted under white law. Recently, some attempts have been made to recognise Aboriginal customary law in the Australian legal system. The Australian Law Reform Commission has also produced a report exploring the relationship between traditional Aboriginal law and Anglo-Australian law.

75 White man's law, 1816 (NLA)
76 Dance of Defiance (NLA)

32

Language

GOVERNOR DAVEY'S
PROCLAMATION
TO THE ABORIGINES
1816

'Why, Massa Governor, said Black Jack - You Proclamation all gammon, how 'Blackfellow read him? Ah! He no learn him read book.'

'Tand that then, said the Governor pointing to a Tablor'

75

76

Before 1788 approximately 270 separate and distinct languages, each with numerous dialects, were spoken in Aboriginal Australia. There may have been as many as 600 to 700 dialects.

Aboriginal languages fall into one of two categories. In one, words inflect for case, tense and mood as in Latin or Greek. In the other, the verb carries information about the person and the number of both its subject and its object. In this it resembles American Indian languages. This latter category of languages is found only in north-western Australia. The other category is found throughout the rest of Australia.

Torres Strait Island languages also fall into one of two categories. People of the eastern islands speak Meriam Mir which is related to, but different from, Papuan languages. Kala Lagaw Y is spoken on the western and central islands. It is related to, but also different from, the Aboriginal languages of Cape York. Distinct dialects of the language are used on different islands.

Aboriginal languages have about twenty sounds, but they do not use all the sounds in English, for example. At the same time they use sounds that are not used in English.

Besides their distinctive sounds, Australian languages have typical grammatical features which give them great flexibility. For instance, they use a range of pronouns which make it possible to include or to exclude the person spoken to in a statement so in Ngandi, an eastern Arnhem Land language, '*njer*' means 'all of us but not you' whilst '*ngorkor*' means 'all of us including you'.

Aboriginal languages are distinctly Australian. Research has not succeeded in

33

linking them to any other language families.

Yet, as languages they compare in every way with other languages spoken by people throughout the world. They are capable of precision, of subtlety, of degrees of emotion and of poetic statement. They have the flexibility to incorporate new concepts and ideas, to name, to describe and to explain new technical items and procedures and to adapt words from other languages.

At least fifty of the more than two hundred original Australian languages are no longer spoken. An insufficient amount of their vocabularies, forms of grammar and pronounciation are now known for them to be revived. There may be a few descendants of original speakers of rare languages who know a few words of it that they might use at home, but this is not enough to preserve or revive a rare language. Until recently, Aborigines were 'encouraged' to abandon their own languages for English.

Another hundred languages have fewer than a hundred speakers, usually much fewer. These languages have not all

Language	Speakers	Comments
1. Kriol	15,000	BE,BT,G,D,LC
2. Torres Strait creole	15,000	
3. Western Desert, eastern:	3,000 + total	
a. Pitjantjatjara	1,000 +	BE,BT,LC
b. Pintupi & Luritja	800 +	BE,BT,C,D,LC
c. Ngaanyatjarra	700	BE,BT,G
d. Gugadja	300	BT
e. Wangkatja	200–300	LC
4. Aranda dialects:	3,00 + total	
a. Western Aranda	1,000?	f&sBE,fBT,LC
b. Eastern Aranda	1,000?	sBE,LC
c. Anmatjirra	800 +	
5. Warlpiri	2,800	BE,BT,G,D,LC
6. Kala Lagaw Ya	2,800?	sBE,f&sBTB
7. Dhuwal-Dhuwala dialects:	1,600–1,700 total	
a. Gupapyunga	450	BE,BT,mLC
b. Gumatj	250–500	BE
c. Djambarrpuyngu	250–450	BE,BT
8. Tiwi	1,400	BE,BT,G
9. Walmatjari	1,300	fBE,BT
10. Anindilyakwa	1,000	fBE,BT
11. Gunwinggu	900	BE,BT,G,mLC
12. Western Desert, western:	900 total	
a. Manyjilyjarra	500	BE,sBT,D
b. Yulbaridja	200?	
c. Martu Wangka	200?	
13. Murrinh-Patha	800 +	BE,sBT
14. Nyangumarta	700–800	BE,sBT
15. Miriam	700?	
16. Yindjibarndi	600 +	
17. Guugu yimidhirr	600	G
18. Burarra	400–600	BT
19. Dhangu dialects:	400 + total	
a. Gaalpu	200	
b. Wangurri	150	BT
20. Alyawarra	400–500	sBT,G
21. Nunggubuyu	300–400	fBE,BT,D
22. Garawa	300–400	BT
23. Wik-Munkan	300 +	BE,BT
24. Kitja	300 +	BT
25. Kuku-Yalanji	300 +	BT
26. Ritharngu	300?	G
27. Gurindji	250	sBT
28. Djaru	250	

Abbreviations

BE	Bilingual education is underway (f = formerly, s = starting)
BT	Bible translation is underway (f = formerly, s = starting)
D	Dictionary has been published
G	Grammar has been published
LC	Language course material is available (m = in manuscript)

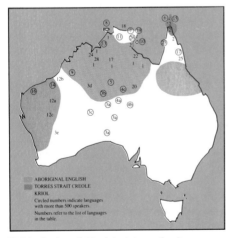

ABORIGINAL ENGLISH
TORRES STRAIT CREOLE
KRIOL
Circled numbers indicate languages with more than 500 speakers.
Numbers refer to the list of languages in the table.

77 Distribution of Aboriginal Australian languages (AIAS)

78 Prominent Aboriginal Australian languages (AIAS)

Oral Tradition and Ceremonies

been recorded fully and current rates of recording are inadequate to save them. For some, when the last speakers of the language die, the language will die with them. Speakers of languages in this category are greatly concerned. They want their languages to survive and be passed on to their children. This is not easy. It takes considerable expertise to record, analyse and document languages to the stage where they can be formally taught. At the same time there is great pressure on 'weak' languages. Their small number of speakers increasingly find themselves having to use 'strong' languages in order to be able to communicate. These 'strong' languages may be other Aboriginal languages, they may be a commonly spoken language like Kriol or they may be English. Children, especially, are under pressure to speak the language of the school, the shop and the radio, which is English, Kriol or another 'strong' Aboriginal language.

Some fifty Aboriginal languages are still regarded as 'strong'. Each is the first language of several hundred speakers and it is generally spoken throughout the day. Often it is used as the beginning language of instruction in schools, and students will become literate and numerate in that language before gaining oracy and literacy skills in English. Some of these languages are also used in radio and television programs broadcast to Aborigines and Islanders in remote communities in Australia. It is very important that these Aboriginal languages which are still spoken and regarded as 'strong' are kept that way for future generations. They are a vital part of Australia's ancient multilingual tradition.

Losing a language is not just to lose a method of communication it is also to lose part of a cultural tradition. This is especially so when, as in the case of Aboriginal languages, the spoken word and the ritual arts are the main means of preserving and transmitting that culture.

All ancient cultures have oral traditions in which the stories of their creation have been carefully preserved. The oral-tradition of Aboriginal and Islander people is still active but, increasingly, efforts are being made to record the traditional stories in writing. The oral traditions are imprinted on the Australian countryside in the form of mountains, hills and lakes. All are natural memorials of the ancient past and are the evidence that the sagas describing the Dreamtime really took place many thousands of years ago. For example, the ancestral creative being Kuniya, the carpet snake, camped and hunted by a waterhole on a large flat sandhill. The sandhill turned to stone and became Uluru (Ayers Rock). Wilkuda, the hunter, threw down the skin of a giant kangaroo that he had killed and it became Lake Eyre. Narran Lake in New South Wales was made by two giant crocodile-like beings as they thrashed about in their death throes. They were hunted and killed by Ba'iame for eating his two young wives. When Djankawu and his two sisters stepped from their canoe on an Arnhem Land beach, the place where they landed became sacred and their canoe, which was turned to stone, is still there to remind people. Pools, hills, jumbled stones, monoliths, lakes, rivers, rocks whose shapes resemble people, animals or familiar objects, stains on rock faces, caves — many are monuments to the ancestral creative beings. Many of them are actual sites where ancestral creative beings still reside and use their powers for good or evil, depending on how well or badly they may be treated.

Other spirit beings, besides the ancestral creative beings, inhabit the Australian countryside. Some are shy spirits that hide themselves away in the dark recesses of rocks, deep caves and water holes. Others are mischievous beings like the *Net-nets* in Victoria who hover just on the border of sight and trip people up and hide things they put down. There are also some other very powerful beings who, although not ancestral beings, have power to intervene in human life. Examples of these are the *Mimi* and *Namorod* spirits of Arnhem Land, the *Quinkans* of Cape York, the *Myndiein* of Victoria and the hairy, man-like spirit of Doolaga found in south coast regions of New South Wales. Children, particularly, are warned to be on the look out for these spirits and they may be threatened with them when they are disobedient.

All of the great ancestral creative beings travelled great distances through the countryside shaping it, leaving pools of unborn spirits and planting and peopling the land. The tracks of these great journeys crisscross the country. The sites of particular events and incidents on these journeys mark the track as it moves from one clan's country to the next.

The storytellers who guard and narrate the events of the ancestral creative beings' journeys can only tell about that part of a journey that occurred in their own land. This is the only part for which they are responsible. No one person will know and therefore be able to tell all the stories that happened on each of the great creation journeys.

Non-Aboriginal writers who set out to retell ancient Aboriginal traditions find that the stories, which relate to particular sites and form part of a series of stories along a particular journey, lose all their real meaning if they are not related to the place they are about and the series of stories to which they belong. Decontextualised and recounted by people who have no authority to tell them, the stories lose their relevance and become no more than imaginary fairytales.

By contrast the ritual performance of a major story cycle reveals the full power and significance of stories, both in terms of a narrative and spiritual meaning. For such a ritual performance a number of clans, which jointly share ownership of stories in the cycle, come together to prepare for and eventually perform the ceremony. The aim of the ritual is to evoke the presence of a specific ancestral creative being and to encourage that being to release again its creative powers. This is achieved by re-enacting in song and dance the events of the great creative saga. Days will be spent in preparation as carvings, paintings, sand sculptures and decorated poles and other ritual items are produced. The standard and accuracy of the art work is carefully scrutinised since anything done poorly or incorrectly may antagonise the ancestral beings. Songs and dances must be rehearsed to make sure that the correct versions are chosen according to the participants and purposes of the particular ceremony. When the ceremony itself begins, the songs and dances follow the same order of travel through the landscape as the original creation journey, but references and links to the lands of the par-

79 80

36

ticipating clans are specially invented. The art objects prepared for the ritual are displayed and introduced at appropriate parts in the ceremony.

This description is deliberately general. The performance of some ritual story cycles are open to all people and they may see the various art objects, watch the dances and hear the songs. Many of these ceremonies, however, like *Kunapipi*, a popular series of ceremonies in Arnhem Land which recall the journeys of Kunapipi, the mother, are secret. These ceremonies are open only to initiated males or females as the case may be. The elements of these performances vary considerably and only the study of each one in detail reveals the ceremony's full meaning.

81

82

Mourning customs

Mourning customs varied throughout Australia, but they always included displays of sorrow and distress.

Burial rites and methods of disposing of the dead were complex and varied, with their main purpose being to ensure the safe return of the spirits of the dead to the spirit home or totemic centre by way of a water hole, the sky or some off-shore island. The rites also safe-guarded the living from the spirits' displeasure and served to avenge the deceased.

There were different methods for disposing of the dead. These included cremation, burial in the ground or in trees, placing the body on free-standing platforms or in caves and rock shelters. Burial rites sometimes involved and still involve prolonged rituals. Often after the remains had decayed they were recovered and burnt, buried, placed in a log coffin, a cave, a rock shelter, a hollow tree, or the branches of a tree.

Pukamani rituals on Melville Island and Bathurst Island were, and still are, long and elaborate. Large groups gather for the final rites. Dancers wear elaborate body decorations and dance events in the life of the deceased person. Large carved and decorated poles are made over the preceding months and erected around the grave during the rites.

79 Male in ceremonial dress (AIAS)

80 Female in ceremonial dress (AOIS)

81 Gubboo Ted Thomas teaching the lore of Mumbulla Mountain, New South Wales (AIAS)

82 Students visiting the battle site at Pinjarra, Western Australia (AII)

83 Traditional ceremony (AOIS)

83

37

Art

Probably the first time that white Australians became conscious of Aborigines as artists was in the late 1940s and 1950s when Albert Namatjira's watercolours of Central Australia captured the attention of the art market. Aborigines and Torres Strait Islanders have always been innovative in their art, both in terms of styles, techniques and materials. By adopting a Western style of painting Namatjira was in fact following an ancient Aboriginal art custom that encouraged experimentation and innovation. Only in religious art, the art produced for use in ritual performance, is there an insistence on maintaining traditional styles and keeping traditional representations.

84

It is generally believed that, like the land, these traditional representations are part of the spiritual inheritance bequeathed to the various clans by the ancestral beings. In the past, and still today in many places, certain art designs may only be seen by initiates attending particular ritual ceremonies. Furthermore, the secret meanings of these sacred paintings can only be revealed to initiates. Although today some of this secrecy has been relaxed and religious paintings are gradually being shown to others, the full significance of the symbols and the deep spirituality of the stories are never revealed.

Aboriginal art began at least 40 000 years ago when ochre was used to paint the corpses of the dead. Body ornaments found in graves attest that body decoration was an ancient tradition as was cave painting and rock engraving. Australia boasts the most extensive and most elaborate series of cave and rock shelter paintings to be found anywhere in the world. These paintings are believed to be the work of the ancestral creative beings. Aboriginal 'curators' pre-serve these paintings by retouching them when the colours fade or when they are damaged. Not all the paintings are quite so ancient, however, for there are fresh hand stencils and paintings of ships, horses, cattle and men with guns that are the work of more recent artists. Many of these newer paintings record the history of initial contact between Aborigines and Europeans.

One recent innovation in Aboriginal art that has proved exceptionally successful was initiated by a non-Aboriginal, Geoffrey Bardon, who was a teacher at Papunya school in Central Australia. He aroused interest among the senior Aboriginal men in the community in 1971 when he asked them for advice on painting a traditional Dreaming story in a school mural. In the end the men themselves took over the mural (*Papunya — Honey Ant Dreaming*) and then were inspired to transfer many of the desert Dreaming stories to board using acrylic paints. Since the traditional desert painting was done in sand using ground

87

85

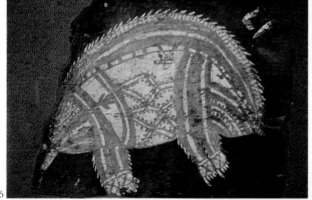

88

86

89

ochre, feathers, hair, string, clay, plant fibre and blood, and since these paintings were prepared for strictly secret men's or women's ceremonies and were always destroyed by the end of it, desert art was mainly ephemeral. The use of board or canvas and acrylic paints made it possible to transfer some of the ceremonial designs onto this more permanent form. Not the strictly sacred ones that only initiated men or only initiated women could see, but those that were open for all to see even though in some cases only the initiated fully understood them. Since each initiated individual inherits rights to a number of public Dreaming stories and designs, there is no limit to the number of paintings that each artist may do. Each artist paints in a

90

84 Painting on bark, Melville Island, Northern Territory (R. Edwards)

85 Stencil paintings, Carnarvon Ranges, Queensland (South Australia Museum)

86 X-ray painting on bark (AOIS)

87 Rock engravings, Hawkesbury District, New South Wales (CA)

88 Carved ceremonial tree, New South Wales (Australian Museum)

89 Specialised application of pigment onto bark, Melville Island (R. Edwards)

90 Preparing bark for painting (All)

39

distinctive way but within the style of their own group.

The names of many desert artists are now well established in the art world and the work of some fetch high prices on the national and international art market.

In the north of Australia traditional art forms are maintained, even though there is also plenty of innovation. Bark paintings were traditionally prepared as an accompaniment to sculptures and carvings for religious ceremonies. They only had life and significance in the ceremony and after the ceremony they were discarded or hidden away. Some very early bark paintings have been preserved in anthropological museum collections and art museums throughout the world. Painting on bark as an art form, however, only really became established from around the 1960s when, under the urging of missionary staff, Aboriginal painters began to sell their bark paintings. To do this they developed techniques for fixing the ochres and clay to the bark and for binding the head and foot of the bark sheets to prevent them from curling.

Like the desert acrylic art, bark paintings that are sold contain only public images that may be seen by all but whose meanings, in many instances, are known fully only to senior men or women. Since bark has to be stripped in sheets from suitable trees, painters have to work with fairly narrow oblong shapes, which affects the stylisation of many of the human/spirit forms or animals and fish that they represent.

Styles vary considerably across the whole of northern Australia and, as with desert artists, the distinctive styles of individual artists and of groups of artists within a family can be recognised. Most of the established painters in this traditional art form also command high prices on the national and international art markets. Though only two painting styles have been mentioned here, Aboriginal artists continue to work in a variety of forms and styles.

Today there are many emerging urban Aboriginal artists who also draw on their ancient art traditions. These artists blend traditional images with the images of their own world and experiences.

Aboriginal and Islander art in all its forms is a tradition which has developed over thousands of years and continues to be a vital and lively means of expression.

91

92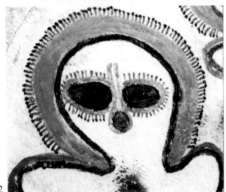

91 Bessie Liddle, an artist from Alice Springs, Northern Territory (AII)

92 Wanjina painting, Kimberley, Western Australia (I.M. Crawford)

40

Becoming Australian

When Australia became a Federation of States in 1901, the Constitution decreed that Aborigines and Islanders were not to be counted as citizens. Each State was responsible for the welfare of its own Aboriginal and Islander populations. As a consequence, Aboriginal and Islander people found themselves subject to a variety of State originated legislation which generally restricted their freedom of movement, and segregated them from other Australians. Sometimes Aboriginal families were torn apart. Children of mixed race ancestry were taken away from their parents and some Aboriginal people were transferred from location to location at the whim of government. They were denied an education that would give them an opportunity to make choices for their own futures. If Aboriginal people were to gain equal status with other white Australians then this depended on their abrogation of their separate cultural identity as Aborigines and Islanders.

In 1967 in an extraordinary demonstration of agreement, white Australian voters in a majority of States said 'Yes' to a proposal to amend the Australian Constitution. The amendment gave all Aborigines and Islanders the status of citizens and gave the Commonwealth responsibility to legislate for them. This meant that while States still had to provide the same services to Aborigines and Islanders as were available to their other citizens, in future their special needs would be identified and legislated for by Federal Government. A new Commonwealth Department of Aboriginal Affairs was set up, and with other Commonwealth departments it became responsible for administering Aboriginal and Islander programs.

94

95

93

93 At the handover of Uluru to traditional owners (AOIS)

94 Emu Farm, Ngangganawili Aboriginal community at Wiluna, Western Australia (AOIS)

95 Stockman (AOIS)

96 Mimi — an Aboriginal-run arts and crafts shop at Katherine, Northern Territory (AII)

96

41

Aborigines and Islanders have been in the forefront of efforts to demand equal rights with other Australians and attonement for the injustices of the last 200 years. They want compensation for the usurpation of their lands and the destruction of their cultural traditions. They also want respect for their human achievement over countless centuries as custodians of Australia. Self-determination, self-management and the acknowledgment of traditional land rights have become the popular claim and the policy of the Commonwealth Government.

Under self-determination, efforts have been made, not always successfully, to involve Aboriginal and Islander people in the decision-making processes of government. Organisations that have influence in shaping government policy — church groups, trade unions, political parties, lobby groups and so on — and policy branches of government departments, have sought to establish representative Aboriginal and Islander advisory and consultative groups so that they may be the ones to determine policy. Decisions on policy and on policy implementation remains in all cases with the legislative and the governing authority of organisations and therefore these advisory and consultative groups do not always succeed in having their recommendations accepted. As a consequence, many Aborigines and Torres Strait Islanders feel that they are still far from achieving self-determination.

Self-management aims to empower Aborigines and Islanders to take over control of their own communities, services and businesses. This policy has led to the establishment of national Aboriginal and Islander organisations in the fields of health and legal aid with the aim of providing health support and legal aid to Aboriginal and Islander people in forms that are culturally acceptable to them. A national federation of Aboriginal and Islander land councils aims to combine the strength, expertise and organisation of the many separate land councils in the States to work towards effective and basically uniform Land Rights legislation for all Aboriginal and Islander peoples. Most States and the Commonwealth have set out to redress some of the injustices done to Aboriginal and Islander people. They have done this by giving them control over what were once church missions or government reserves, by returning to them land to which they are entitled in legislation to lay claim, and by helping them to purchase properties available on the open market. Some States have allocated funds for dispersal to community groups, land councils and Aboriginal and Islander organisations to help in establishing enterprises or meeting their needs for housing, schooling, higher education and training, employment and other community identified projects.

No government, no social researcher, and certainly no Aboriginal or Islander person would claim that Aborigines and Islanders have yet overcome their devastating experiences of the last 200 years. However, they continue to work towards the day when there is no longer a need for governments to legislate especially for them, when the wrongs done to them have been redressed as far as they ever may be, and when they know that they are confidently in charge of their own lives and affairs.

97 Outstation near Hermannsberg, Central Australia (AII)